THE
A-Z
OF WONDER
WOMEN

YVONNE LIN

Little, Brown and Company

New York Boston

CONTENTS

—

INTRODUCTION

—

This book is an illustrated alphabet of outstanding women.

The stories of their lives will inspire women everywhere, but in particular they will spark our kids as they grow up. My own little girl, Roni, is almost four years old now. Every day she doubts, tries, stumbles, and achieves. She grows. Watching her, her friends, and little girls on the street, I can't help but think about their future. Will they only dream, or will they succeed? What will keep them back? What can we do to help them reach their full power?

Girls and boys need heroes as they grow up. They play with action figures, watch movies, and read books. There are thousands upon thousands of books and movies about famous athletes, scientists, artists, and explorers—but they're almost all men. Whatever a little boy wants to pursue, he sees the paths to success.

Who are Roni's role models? Girls get princesses and mermaids—sure, not necessarily the worst career choices, but there are not enough castles and beaches for the world's 3.5 billion women.

When women do excel in fields other than princess-ing and mermaid-ing, their accomplishments get pink-washed. Florence Nightingale becomes known as a sweet nurse who holds soldiers' hands through the night, rather than a statistician and analyst. Of all the Disney films, Roni loves *Mulan* best, a story about a girl who ran away from home, chopped off her hair, dressed as a man, joined the army, saved China from the invading Mongols, and became a war hero. But Mulan dolls only come with long flowing hair and a glittery ball gown.

Adults may not say these messages out loud, but kids see them day after day. Their futures and choices are introduced and reinforced again and again. It doesn't have to be this way. I created my book and populated it with twenty-six outstanding women from *A* to *Z* to show kids how much women have achieved, even against overwhelming odds.

Roni and her friends will learn that little girls grew up and flew to the moon; won the highest prizes in science and math; led countries, armies, and even pirate fleets; became billionaires and created Harry Potter.

I am more of an artist than a writer, so this book has more drawings than words. I hope readers will look at these women and imagine how they fought and succeeded. They are Aboriginal, Asian, African, white, young, old, strong, smart, harsh, kind, and stubborn. They show that there is no one way to be a woman, or to succeed. And they make me proud.

I owe it to these women to bring them out of the shadows that history exiled them to. They will shine the light on the paths to success for our kids.

IS FOR ADA, ACE OF ALGORITHMS.

Ada Lovelace (1815–1852) was an English mathematician. She recognized the potential of the modern computer and wrote the first punch-card algorithm a century before the modern computer age. Ada was the first computer programmer.

B

IS FOR BENAZIR, BREAKER OF BOUNDARIES.

Benazir Bhutto (1953–2007) was the first democratically elected female leader of a Muslim country. She served two terms as the prime minister of Pakistan. She was a champion of women's rights.

C

IS FOR CATHY, CHASER OF CHAMPIONS.

Cathy Freeman (1973–) is the first Aboriginal Commonwealth Games gold medal winner. After winning the 400 meters at the 2000 Summer Olympics, she took a victory lap carrying both the Australian and Aboriginal flags—despite the fact that unofficial national flags are banned at the Olympic Games.

> "
>
> THIS WAS MY RACE AND NO ONE WAS GOING TO STOP ME TELLING THE WORLD HOW PROUD I WAS TO BE ABORIGINAL.
>
> "
>
> CATHY FREEMAN

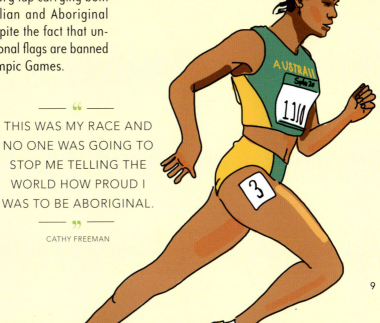

D

IS FOR DOROTHEA, DOCUMENTER OF THE DEPRESSION.

Dorothea Lange (1895–1965) was an American photojournalist. Her iconic photographs exposed the plight of sharecroppers, displaced farmers, and migrant workers during the Great Depression in the 1930s. She showed the power of documentary photography.

> "
> THE CAMERA IS AN INSTRUMENT THAT TEACHES PEOPLE HOW TO SEE WITHOUT A CAMERA.
> "
>
> DOROTHEA LANGE

$$j^\nu \quad \frac{\partial \psi \cdot}{\partial x^\mu} \psi \Big) \eta^{\nu\mu}$$

E

IS FOR EMMY, ENCHANTER OF EQUATIONS.

Emmy Noether (1882–1935) was a German-American mathematician. Albert Einstein called her "the most significant creative mathematical genius thus far produced since the higher education of women began." Emmy devised Noether's theorem, which laid the foundation for quantum physics

IS FOR FLORENCE, FIGHTER OF FILTH.

Florence Nightingale (1820–1910) was an English statistician and the founder of modern nursing. Her statistics work has saved countless lives. She discovered that poor sanitary practices were the main cause of death in hospitals, and devised new hygienic practices.

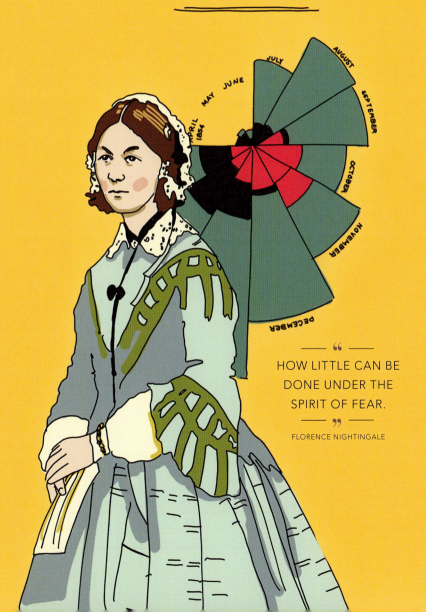

DIAGRAM of the CAUSES of MORTALITY in the ARMY in the EAST.

> " HOW LITTLE CAN BE DONE UNDER THE SPIRIT OF FEAR. "
>
> FLORENCE NIGHTINGALE

G

IS FOR GRACE, GUTSY GAL OF THE GALLEON.

Grace O'Malley (1530–1603) was an ambitious Irish pirate queen. Grace and her crew dominated the coast of Ireland, raiding merchant ships, conquering castles from rival clans, and battling English armies.

> "
> SHE HAD STRONGHOLDS
> ON HER HEADLANDS
> AND BRAVE GALLEYS
> ON THE SEA
> AND NO WARLIKE
> CHIEF OR VIKING
> E'ER HAD BOLDER
> HEART THAN SHE.
> "
>
> FROM THE SONG
> "GRANUAILE"

H

IS FOR HARRIET, HIKER OF THE HIGHLANDS.

I'VE NEVER FOUND MY SEX A HINDERMENT; NEVER FACED A DIFFICULTY WHICH A WOMAN, AS WELL AS A MAN, COULD NOT SURMOUNT.

HARRIET CHALMERS ADAMS

Harriet Chalmers Adams (1875–1937) was an American explorer. She traveled more than 100,000 miles, discovering Incan ruins, canoeing the Amazon, and traversing the Andes. She met twenty indigenous tribes, likely more than any white woman at the time. She shared her stories in _National Geographic_ and was one of the most popular adventure lecturers of the early twentieth century.

> I WAS BROUGHT UP TO
> BELIEVE THAT A PERSON
> MUST BE RESCUED WHEN
> DROWNING, REGARDLESS OF
> RELIGION AND NATIONALITY.

IRENA SENDLER

I

IS FOR IRENA,
INTREPID SAVIOR
OF INFANTS.

Irena Sendler (1910–2008) was a
Polish nurse and humanitarian.
Irena and her coworkers smug-
gled approximately 2,500 Jewish
children out of the Warsaw Ghetto.
They provided the children with
false identity documents and
shelter. Irena directly saved more
Jews than any other individual
during the Holocaust.

IS FOR J. K., JUVENILE JOY BRINGER.

J. K. Rowling (1965–) is a British writer. Despite its being rejected by the first twelve publishers, *Harry Potter and the Sorcerer's Stone* started a literary revolution. Millions of formerly reluctant young readers have eagerly read all 4,224 pages of her Harry Potter books.

> IT MATTERS NOT
> WHAT SOMEONE IS
> BORN, BUT WHAT
> THEY GROW TO BE!

J. K. ROWLING

IS FOR KATE, KEEN CAPTAIN OF WOMANKIND.

Kate Sheppard (1847–1934) was the leader of the New Zealand suffragettes. She wrote pamphlets, edited the first woman-operated newspaper, and helped gather 30,000 signatures in a petition that was presented to Parliament. As a result, in 1893, New Zealand became the first country to give women the right to vote.

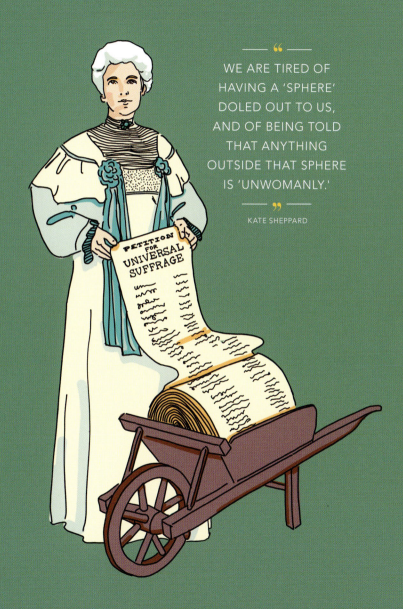

> "WE ARE TIRED OF HAVING A 'SPHERE' DOLED OUT TO US, AND OF BEING TOLD THAT ANYTHING OUTSIDE THAT SPHERE IS 'UNWOMANLY.'
>
> KATE SHEPPARD

PETITION FOR UNIVERSAL SUFFRAGE

L

IS FOR LYDA, LEADER OF THE LAW.

> " IN THIS CEMETERY ARE BURIED ONE-HUNDRED OF OUR ANCESTORS...WHY SHOULD WE NOT BE PROUD OF OUR ANCESTORS AND PROTECT THEIR GRAVES? "
>
> LYDA CONLEY

Lyda Conley (1869–1946) was a Wyandot-American lawyer. She was the first Native American woman to bring a case before the US Supreme Court. Lyda was the first person to argue that Native American burying grounds are entitled to federal protection.

M

IS FOR MARIA, MASTER OF MONTESSORI.

Maria Montessori (1870–1952) was one of Italy's first female physicians and a trailblazing education innovator. Maria designed teaching materials and a classroom environment that builds on the way children naturally learn, and she opened the first Montessori school.

———— " ————

THIS IS OUR MISSION: TO CAST A RAY OF LIGHT AND PASS ON.

———— " ————

MARIA MONTESSORI

23

N

IS FOR NELLIE, NERVY NARRATOR OF THE NAKED TRUTH.

Nellie Bly (1864–1922), born Elizabeth Cochrane Seaman, was an American investigative journalist and adventurer. She posed as a mental patient to expose the conditions of asylum patients on Blackwell's Island. Nellie's work changed public policy, her outfits influenced fashion trends, and her adventures inspired board games.

> I TOOK UPON MYSELF TO
> ENACT THE PART OF A POOR,
> UNFORTUNATE CRAZY
> GIRL, AND FELT IT MY DUTY
> NOT TO SHIRK ANY OF THE
> DISAGREEABLE RESULTS THAT
> SHOULD FOLLOW.

NELLIE BLY

66

KNOW WHAT SPARKS THE
LIGHT IN YOU. THEN USE THAT
LIGHT TO ILLUMINATE THE WORLD.

99

OPRAH WINFREY

IS FOR OPRAH, OPENHEARTED ORATORY POWERHOUSE.

Oprah Winfrey (1954–) is an American media mogul. She was born into a poor family in rural Mississippi. From her humble beginnings, she worked her way up to become North America's first African-American multibillionaire and one of the most influential women of her generation.

IS FOR PATSY, PREJUDICE-OPPOSED POLITICIAN.

Patsy T. Mink (1927–2002) was an American politician who fought against gender and racial discrimination. She was the first non-white woman elected to Congress. She cowrote, sponsored, and secured the passage of Title IX, which prohibited gender discrimination by federally funded institutions.

> IT IS EASY ENOUGH TO VOTE RIGHT AND BE CONSISTENTLY WITH THE MAJORITY. BUT IT IS MORE OFTEN MORE IMPORTANT TO BE AHEAD OF THE MAJORITY AND THIS MEANS BEING WILLING TO CUT THE FIRST FURROW IN THE GROUND AND STAND ALONE FOR A WHILE IF NECESSARY.

PATSY T. MINK

Q

IS FOR QIU, QUICK-FOOTED AND QUOTABLE FEMINIST FIGHTER.

Qiu Jin (1875–1907) was a Chinese revolutionary, feminist, and writer. She founded a newspaper in which she spoke out for women's rights, including freedom from oppressive marriages, education, and the abolishment of foot binding. And she was a martial artist who trained an army of female revolutionaries.

> " DON'T TELL ME WOMEN ARE NOT THE STUFF OF HEROES. "
>
> QIU JIN

R

IS FOR RUTH, ROBED IN REASON.

Ruth Bader Ginsburg (1933–) is the second female justice on the US Supreme Court. She is an advocate for the advancement of gender equality and women's rights. Before becoming a judge, Ruth cofounded the Women's Rights Project at the ACLU and argued six gender discrimination cases before the Supreme Court, winning five.

> I AM A WOMAN WHO CAME
> FROM THE COTTON FIELDS
> OF THE SOUTH. I WAS
> PROMOTED FROM
> THERE TO THE WASHTUB.
> THEN I WAS PROMOTED TO
> THE COOK KITCHEN.
> AND FROM THERE I PROMOTED
> MYSELF INTO THE BUSINESS OF
> MANUFACTURING HAIR GOODS
> AND PREPARATIONS....I HAVE
> BUILT MY OWN FACTORY ON MY
> OWN GROUND.

SARAH BREEDLOVE

S

IS FOR SARAH,
SELF-MADE
MILLIONAIRE OF
STUNNING HAIR.

Sarah Breedlove (1867–1919), also known as Madam C. J. Walker, was the first American female self-made millionaire. She amassed her fortune by developing and marketing a line of beauty and hair products for black women. She also showed women how to budget and build their own businesses, and encouraged them to become financially independent.

T

IS FOR TINA, TITILLATING TICKLER.

Tina Fey (1970–) is an American comedian and producer. She became *Saturday Night Live*'s first female head writer. Since then, she has written and starred in movies and TV shows, including *Mean Girls* and *30 Rock*.

—— " ——

YOU CAN'T BE THAT KID
STANDING AT THE TOP
OF THE WATERSLIDE,
OVERTHINKING IT.
YOU HAVE TO GO
DOWN THE CHUTE.

—— " ——

TINA FEY

U

IS FOR URSULA, UNBOUND AUTHOR OF UNCOMMON WORLDS.

Ursula K. Le Guin (1929–2018) was an American writer. She won every science fiction award possible, most more than once. Ursula's fully imagined worlds challenge readers to question conventions of gender, race, the environment, and society.

> **"**
>
> MY IMAGINATION MAKES ME HUMAN AND MAKES ME A FOOL; IT GIVES ME ALL THE WORLD, AND EXILES ME FROM IT.
>
> **99**
>
> URSULA K. LE GUIN

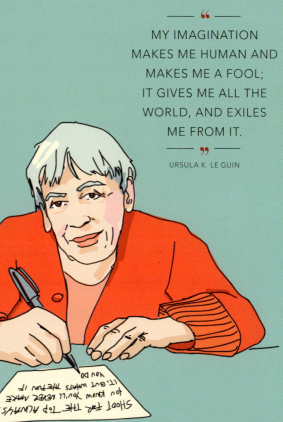

IS FOR VALENTINA, VANGUARD SPACE VOYAGER.

Valentina Tereshkova (1937–) is a Russian cosmonaut and engineer. As a young woman, she skydived as a hobby, and in 1963 she became the first woman in space. She orbited Earth forty-eight times. In 2013, she offered to go on a one-way trip to Mars.

ON EARTH, MEN AND WOMEN
ARE TAKING THE SAME RISKS.
WHY SHOULDN'T WE BE TAKING
THE SAME RISKS IN SPACE?

VALENTINA TERESHKOVA

IS FOR WAJEHA, WISE WARRIOR FOR WOMEN.

Wajeha al-Huwaider (1962–) is a Saudi activist. She campaigns against laws that give men control over women. In 2008, when women in Saudi Arabia were banned from driving, she filmed herself driving and posted it on YouTube. In 2013, she was sentenced to ten months in prison for attempting to help a woman escape her abusive husband.

> "
> SAUDI WOMEN ARE WEAK,
> NO MATTER HOW HIGH THEIR STATUS,
> EVEN THE 'PAMPERED' ONES AMONG THEM—
> BECAUSE THEY HAVE NO LAW TO PROTECT
> THEM FROM ATTACK BY ANYONE.
> "
> WAJEHA AL-HUWAIDER

X

IS FOR XUE, XENACIOUS EXPLORER OF THE UNHEARD.

Xue Xinran (1958–) is a Chinese-British journalist. She shocked China when she broke taboos and created a radio show to tell the heartbreaking and never-before-heard stories from women about forced marriages, child abuse, foot binding, and oppression. She was eventually forced to leave China because of her brave storytelling.

> "
> I DISCOVERED THAT
> WOMEN HAD NO
> IDEA HOW TO TALK
> ABOUT THEMSELVES.
> "
>
> XUE XINRAN

Y

IS FOR YAYOI, YARDS OF YUMMY DOTS.

Yayoi Kusama (1929–) is a wild and eccentric Japanese artist. Her work influenced Andy Warhol, David Hockney, and Keith Haring. She creates sculptures, paintings, and dizzying and dazzling polka-dot-filled walk-in installations.

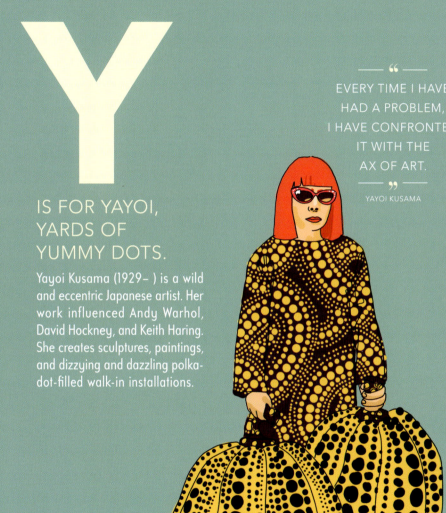

IS FOR ZAHA, ZESTFULLY ZANY ARCHITECT.

Zaha Hadid (1950–2016) was an Iraqi-British architect. Known as the "Queen of the Curve," she created breathtakingly expressive buildings. She was the first woman to receive the Pritzker Architecture Prize.

I DON'T THINK
THAT ARCHITECTURE IS
ONLY ABOUT SHELTER....
IT SHOULD BE ABLE TO
EXCITE YOU, TO CALM YOU,
TO MAKE YOU THINK.

ZAHA HADID

22

MORE WONDER WOMEN

Selecting just twenty-six wonder women to include in this book was a difficult task—so I'm making room for twenty-two more here. These women redefined gender roles, fought poverty, climbed mountains, saved lives, and more. They are inspiring, amazing, and awesome.

ANGELA MERKEL (1954–), the chancellor of Germany since 2005, is one of the most powerful women in the world. She often acts as the leader of the European Union.

BOUDICCA (30 AD–61 AD) was a Celtic warrior queen who led a rebellion in Britain against the occupying Roman Empire. Boudicca's warriors obliterated the Roman Ninth Legion.

CHIEN-SHIUNG WU (1912–1997) was a nuclear physicist. She was a Princeton University faculty member before women were admitted, and she designed an experiment known as the Wu experiment, for which her colleagues were awarded the Nobel Prize.

CHING SHIH (1775–1844) was the most successful pirate of all time. She controlled the China Sea with a fleet of 1,500 ships and 80,000 sailors and created a strict code of pirate law with special protections for female captives.

GERTRUDE B. ELION (1918–1999) was a biochemist who won the Nobel Prize in medicine for creating AZT, the drug that prevents and treats HIV and AIDS. She also developed antirejection medications that are used to treat organ-transplant patients.

HARRIET TUBMAN (c. 1820–1913) escaped slavery in the North in 1849. She made nineteen trips to the South, leading three hundred slaves to freedom in the North.

JACINDA ARDERN (1980–) is prime minister of New Zealand. She was elected at thirty-seven, making her the world's youngest female head of government. She has reached out to the underserved indigenous Māori communities.

JANE GOODALL (1934–) is the world's leading expert on chimpanzees. Jane spent fifty-five years studying and living with wild chimpanzees in Tanzania and now advocates for ecological conservation and animal welfare.

JEANNE BARÉ (1740–1807) was the first woman to travel around the world. Since women were not permitted on official expedition ships, she disguised herself as a man and enlisted as a valet.

JULIA GILLARD (1961–) was the first (and so far only) female prime minister of Australia. She led the country from 2010 to 2013 and recently launched the Global Institute for Women's Leadership to get more women into leadership roles around the world.

LHAKPA SHERPA (1973–) holds the world record for summits of Everest by a woman. She has already climbed the mountain eight times! Lhakpa also works as a dishwasher at a Whole Foods in Connecticut so that her daughters can go to the best schools.

MAE JEMISON (1956–) entered Stanford University at sixteen. After graduating, she went to Cornell Medical College and worked as a Peace Corps doctor in Sierra Leone and Liberia. She went on to become the first African American female astronaut.

MALALA YOUSAFZAI (1997–) is a girls' education activist and the youngest-ever Nobel Prize winner. At eleven, she started writing a blog advocating for girls' education in Pakistan under Taliban rule. At fifteen, she was shot by the Taliban in retaliation.

MARY WOLLSTONECRAFT (1759–1797) was one of the first feminist philosophers. In *A Vindication of the Rights of Woman*, she writes that women should not be treated like ornaments or property and that they deserve the same rights as men.

MARYAM MIRZAKHANI (1977–2017) was the first woman to win the Fields Medal, the most prestigious mathematics award in the world. As a teenager, she and her friend Roya Beheshti were the first two girls on Iran's Mathematical Olympiad team.

MISTY COPELAND (1982–) is the first African American woman to be a principal dancer in the American Ballet Theatre, one of the leading classical ballet companies in the United States.

NANCY WAKE (1912–2011) was a French spy during the Second World War. In 1943, Nancy was at the top of the Gestapo's most-wanted list—they put a 5-million-franc price on her head.

NESS KNIGHT (1985–) is a South African endurance adventurer. She ran fifteen marathons in fifteen days, crossed the Namib Desert alone, swam the Thames River from its source to London, and cycled across Bolivia with no money.

NOOR INAYAT KHAN (1914–1944) was Britain's first Muslim war heroine. She was the first female radio operator secret agent, an incredibly dangerous job. The average tenure of the job was six weeks, and Noor lasted almost four months.

TOMOE GOZEN (twelfth century) was a samurai warrior. In the medieval epic *The Tale of the Heike*, it was written that "so dexterously did she handle sword and bow that she was a match for a thousand warriors."

VIGDÍS FINNBOGADÓTTIR (1930–) was the first woman in the world to be elected president in a democratic election. She became president of Iceland in 1980 and was reelected three times. She fought for parental leave and to close the gender pay gap.

WANG ZHENYI (1768–1797) was a Chinese scientist and mathematician at a time when almost no women were educated. She wrote at least twelve books, on subjects such as the Pythagorean theorem, trigonometry, and solar eclipses.

QUOTE SOURCES

Ada Lovelace: In her letter to Charles Babbage, July 1843.

Benazir Bhutto: Michael Collopy, ed., "Reflections on Working Toward Peace," *Architects of Peace: Visions of Hope in Words and Images* (New World Library: Novato, CA, 2000).

Cathy Freeman: Linda K. Fuller, *Sexual Sports Rhetoric* (Peter Lang Inc.: New York, 2009).

Dorothea Lange: Milton Meltzer, *Dorothea Lange: A Photographer's Life* (Syracuse University Press: New York, 1978).

Emmy Noether: In her letter to Helmut Hasse, 1931, in Auguste Dick, *Emmy Noether, 1882–1935* (Birkhäuser Verlag: Basel, 1981).

Florence Nightingale: Sir Edward Cook, *The Life of Florence Nightingale*, Vol. I (1820–1861) (Macmillan: London, 1913).

Grace O'Malley: Anne Chambers, *Granuaile: Grace O'Malley—Ireland's Pirate Queen* (Gill & Macmillan: Dublin, 2009).

Harriet Chalmers Adams: "Woman Explorer's Hazardous Trip in South America," *New York Times* (August 18, 1912).

Irena Sendler: Adam Easton, "Holocaust Heroine's Survival Tale," *BBC News* (March 3, 2005).

J. K. Rowling: Rowling, *Harry Potter and the Goblet of Fire* (Scholastic: New York, 2000).

Kate Sheppard: Paul Stanley Ward, "Kate Sheppard: Suffragist," *NZEDGE* (May 26, 2000).

Lyda Conley: *Kansas City Times* (October 25, 1906).

Maria Montessori: Montessori, *The Discovery of the Child* (Aakar Books: Delhi, 2004).

Nellie Bly: Bly, *Ten Days in a Mad-House* (Ian L. Munro: New York, 1887).

Oprah Winfrey: Oprah.com, quote from Bold Moves mobile game.

Patsy T. Mink: *Honolulu Star-Bulletin* (October 8, 1975).

Qiu Jin: From her poem "Capping Rhymes with Sir Shih Ching from Sun's Root Land."

Ruth Bader Ginsburg: Melanie Arter, "Justice Ginsburg: We Need an All-Female Supreme Court," *CNS News* (November 26, 2012).

Sarah Breedlove: Henry Louis Gates, Jr., "Madam C.J. Walker: Her Crusade," *Time* (December 7, 1998).

Tina Fey: Fey, "Lessons from Late Night: What Separates the Women from the Men," *New Yorker* (March 14, 2011).

Ursula K. Le Guin: Le Guin, "Winged: The Creatures on My Mind," *Harper's* (August 1990).

Valentina Tereshkova: Pallab Ghosh, "Valentina Tereshkova: USSR Was 'Worried' about Women in Space," *BBC News* (September 17, 2015).

Wajeha al-Huwaider: Aluma Dankowitz, "Saudi Writer and Journalist Wajeha al-Huwaider Fights for Women's Rights," *Memri* (December 28, 2006).

Xue Xinran: Emine Saner, "Xinran: Top 100 Women: Art, Film, Music, and Fashion," *Guardian* (March 7, 2011).

Yayoi Kusama: From her manifesto, as quoted in Leslie Camhi, "Women on the Verge," *Village Voice* (July 14, 1998).

Zaha Hadid: Blake Gopnik, "Design Diva Hits a High Z: Zaha Hadid," *Newsweek*, September 21, 2011.

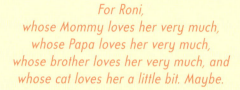

For Roni,
whose Mommy loves her very much,
whose Papa loves her very much,
whose brother loves her very much, and
whose cat loves her a little bit. Maybe.

About This Book: The illustrations for this book were done digitally. This book was edited by Kheryn Callender and designed by Yvonne Lin and Nicole Brown. The production was supervised by Virginia Lawther, and the production editor was Jen Graham. The text was set in Universalis ADF, and the display type is Avenir.

Simultaneously published in 2018 by Hachette Children's Group in the UK • First US Edition: December 2018 • Little, Brown and Company is a division of Hachette Book Group, Inc. • The Little, Brown name and logo are trademarks of Hachette Book Group, Inc. • The publisher is not responsible for websites (or their content) that are not owned by the publisher. • Library of Congress Cataloging-in-Publication Data • Names: Lin, Yvonne, author. • Title: The A-Z of wonder women / Yvonne Lin. • Description: First edition. | New York : Little, Brown and Company, [2018] Identifiers: LCCN 2018013876| ISBN 9780316420976 (hardcover) | ISBN 9780316420969 (ebook) | ISBN 9780316421027 (library edition ebook) • Subjects: LCSH: Women—Biography—Juvenile literature. | Women—History—Juvenile literature. | Alphabet books. • Classification: LCC HQ1123 .L56 2018 | DDC 920.72—dc23 • LC record available at https://lccn.loc.gov/2018013876 • ISBNs: 978-0-316-42097-6 (hardcover), 978-0-316-42096-9 (ebook), 978-0-316-48782-5 (ebook), 978-0-316-48780-1 (ebook) • PRINTED IN MALAYSIA • IM • 10 9 8 7 6 5 4 3 2 1

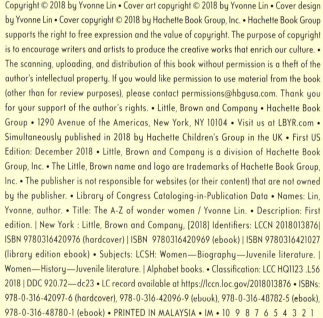
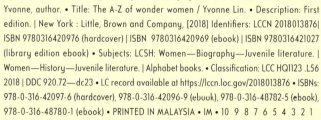